Original title:
Shimmering in the Tropics

Copyright © 2025 Creative Arts Management OÜ
All rights reserved.

Author: Sebastian Whitmore
ISBN HARDBACK: 978-1-80581-573-0
ISBN PAPERBACK: 978-1-80581-100-8
ISBN EBOOK: 978-1-80581-573-0

Pathway to the Gentle Caress

Watch your step on this soft path,
Where flip-flops dance and giggles laugh.
Sun shines bright, but oh so hot,
Socks and sandals? A funny plot!

Lizards skitter, doing the twist,
Geckos gossip, they can't be missed.
Palm trees sway with sass and flair,
They wave out loud like they just don't care!

Dreams Adrift on Coconut Winds

Coconuts roll like bowling balls,
Serving shade through the sun's high calls.
Dreams drift high on this warm breeze,
Sipping coconut water with ease!

Squirrels plot in trees up high,
Wearing shades as they giggle and pry.
The island life, a wild ride,
Where every crab thinks it's a slide!

Nature's Lullaby in a Tropical Night

Stars wink down through the palms above,
While frogs croak songs of unrequited love.
The fireflies blink like tiny lamps,
As night moves in with cheeky pranks.

Tropical breezes tickle your nose,
While iguanas strike silly poses.
A hammock sways, a ropey delight,
But watch for falls in the deep moonlight!

Kaleidoscope of Colors and Life

Vibrant blooms in a rainbow parade,
Butterflies fluttering, feeling well-played.
The parrot squawks, "I'm the best dressed!"
And a crab in a tutu gets quite the jest!

Turtles wobble on sandy shores,
Making a splash as everyone roars.
A dance-off beneath the glowing sun,
Where even the fish join in for fun!

Dappled Light on Sandy Paths

Sunshine dances on the shore,
While crabs wear hats, oh what a bore!
The seagulls squawk a silly flight,
Chasing shadows, oh what a sight!

Umbrella drinks with silly straws,
A beach ball bounces, breaking laws.
The sunburnt skin, a lobster red,
Just makes you want to jump in bed!

Enchanted Isles of Serenity

Coconuts giggle from their trees,
As monkeys swing and catch the breeze.
Island tunes with ukuleles,
Dance with waves, making us jellies!

Tiki torches flicker in the night,
While critters call out in delight.
Grass skirts twirl with wobbly feet,
Join the party—can't be beat!

Flavors of the Ocean's Heart

Fish tacos float like boats in air,
Plankton jump, with no sign of care.
Shrimp on skewers strike a pose,
As pineapple rings do their shows!

Jellyfish jiggle in delight,
Salsa dances with newfound bite.
Tasty waves crash on our plates,
Laughter bursts, oh what great mates!

The Golden Embrace of Dawn

Golden rays tickle sleepy eyes,
As crickets trade in their night cries.
Bacon sizzles—what a surprise,
While lizards pose in morning skies!

Seabirds gossip on the sand,
With fishy tales of sunbaked land.
Morning coffee spills like dreams,
The day unfolds in laughing beams!

Enchanted Isles Under Moonlight

On an island where the coconuts dance,
The crabs wear sunglasses with a silly glance.
Flipping pancakes in the sand,
The seagulls join in, a breakfast band.

Turtles strut in their fancy hats,
Debating the best spots for sunny chats.
Under the moonlight, they shimmy and sway,
Cracking jokes till the break of day.

Lustrous Rainforest Melodies

Amidst the trees, the monkeys play tunes,
Swinging and leaping like playful cartoons.
Parrots gossip in squawky tones,
While sloths take selfies on their phones.

Frogs croak operas from lily pads near,
Their melodies making every critter cheer.
The snake cracks jokes, funny and sly,
As the whole forest laughs—oh my, oh my!

Shining Palettes of Paradise

In a world where colors frolic and blend,
The flowers giggle as they twist and bend.
Butterflies paint with strokes so bold,
While the bees tell tales of their honey gold.

A parrot struts in a sequined vest,
Declaring loudly, "I'm the garden's best!"
The sunflowers nod, with faces that beam,
As they waltz together in a dream.

Opalescent Skies at Sunset

As the sun dips low, the clouds get a tease,
The flamingos prance with the greatest of ease.
The horizon giggles in hues so bright,
While the fish flash smiles, gleaming in light.

Stars begin to twinkle with cheeky grins,
The crickets chirp like they're starting bands.
The night teases softly with a wink and a sigh,
In this playful paradise where laughter won't die.

Twinkling Stars Above Tropical Shores

Beneath the sky of midnight blue,
The crabs wear shades, oh, who knew?
They dance on sand, not missing a beat,
While fish-watching folks just can't find their seat.

A coconut falls with a comedic thud,
Splitting asunder, a drink's massive flood!
The moonlight giggles as waves swirl and sway,
While parrots squawk jokes till the break of day.

Brilliance in the Breeze

With every gust, the leaves start to shiver,
As the toucan flies and does a nifty quiver.
The hammock's a boat on waves of good times,
While lizards mumble their funny old rhymes.

A pineapple wears a hat just for fun,
While the sun proves it's hotter than any ol' gun.
Monkeys swing by, throwing coconuts down,
Their laughter rings loud in this tropical town.

Mosaic of Colorful Flora

In gardens where colors blend and collide,
A flower whispers secrets, with petals as pride.
The bees wear tuxedos to party and dance,
While a cactus rolls by, lost in a trance.

Bright blooms gossip about the sun's tan,
While the daffodils ask, "Where's the nearest can?"
Every petal's a comedian, hoping to shine,
In a comedy show where the sun's the divine.

Delight of Daybreak in Eden

As dawn tosses hues in a playful embrace,
The roosters debate who's the best in the race.
A zephyr brings laughter, a teasing delight,
While the sloths make a pun about staying up late.

The sun yawns wide, stretching its warm glow,
While the flora clap hands for the show.
Bright oranges, pinks, lighting up the day,
In a paradise circus, come join the parade!

A Radiant Touch of Paradise

Beneath the palm, a coconut falls,
A surprise for the one who sprawls.
Sipping drinks with a silly grin,
Laughing loudly, let the fun begin.

Flip-flops dance on sandy floors,
While crabs march close to ocean shores.
Parrots squawk with colorful flair,
As every moment is filled with air.

Kites high up, like dreams set free,
Chasing shadows, come play with me.
Sunburns map adventures untold,
In this land where laughter is bold.

With every wave, a giggle swells,
And fish parade in aquatic spells.
Joy is the sunscreen for every heart,
In this paradise, we'll never part.

Ethereal Gardens of Coral and Coral

Underwater worlds, oh what a sight,
With fish that flash, they giggle in flight.
Coral castles in vibrant hues,
Dance with the rhythm, in oceanic blues.

Octopus plays peek-a-boo so sly,
While sea turtles float gently by.
Starfish lounge, with arms spread wide,
In this garden where giggles reside.

Tropical fish wear silly hats,
As we join in, embracing the chats.
Anemones sway to a song so sweet,
As snorkels tickle and fins tap feet.

In this realm of wonder and glee,
Every creature shares joy, can't you see?
Together we splash, with bubbles and cheer,
In a paradise that draws us near.

Heartbeats Underneath the Shade

In the shade where the bananas hang,
We hear the laughter of a clang.
A monkey steals our lunch away,
While we toast with drinks, let's play all day!

The breeze carries a tickle and tease,
As we chase squirrels with trunks of cheese.
Picnic spreads become slippery slides,
In this shady realm, our silliness abides.

Grasshoppers jump with a comic flair,
As we dance like no one's aware.
Under leafy canopies, we have fun,
Beneath the sun who never shuns.

In cozy corners where hearts can play,
We'll dance through the night and brighten the day.
Every heartbeat, a rhythm so bold,
Creating stories that never grow old.

Guided by the Flicker of Fireflies

As dusk descends, the magic ignites,
With fireflies joining the playful sights.
Chasing lights that twinkle and dart,
Creating a glow in every heart.

Lanterns sway on the porch out front,
As laughter erupts in a joyous hunt.
Cicadas play a concert bizarre,
While stars peek down to see who we are.

In the stillness, a dance takes flight,
Every giggle shines, oh what a sight!
With jars in hand, we capture the day,
In this silly dance, we'll laugh and sway.

As the woods join in our playful song,
We'll frolic and prance, the night feels so long.
United in joy with a flickering cheer,
In this sweet moment, we hold each dear.

Dance of the Tropical Breeze

Palm trees sway as if they dance,
With the breeze that gives them a chance.
Coconuts drop in a comical way,
While tourists munch on chips all day.

Flip-flops flip with every step,
While sunburned noses can barely prep.
Laughter floats on the salty air,
As seagulls steal snacks without a care.

Silhouettes Against the Setting Sun

Shadows stretch like sleepy cats,
On beach towels and sunken mats.
As the sun slides down with a grin,
A game of frisbee's about to begin.

Kids run wild, dodging waves,
While ice cream melts and mischief braves.
Flip a crab, hear the cheers erupt,
It's hard to keep sand from getting plumped!

Radiant Mirage Over the Lagoon

Reflections flicker like fish on patrol,
While snorkelers chase bubbles without control.
Turtles peek, with a knowing glance,
Thinking, 'Why the fuss? Let's dance!'

Kayaks clash like clumsy brew,
As paddlers giggle with things askew.
A fish thinks it's fashionably late,
Turns out it just loves to fluctuate.

Blooming Colors of the Coast

Flowers are loud, like a fiesta parade,
While bees buzz about, quite unafraid.
Sun hats tip over on heads so bald,
And laughter escapes from the beach ball's hold.

Surfers collide, then shout with glee,
Wipeouts are just free entertainment, you see!
With each wave they tumble and flip,
Making this coast a hilarious trip.

Essence of the Exuberant Rainforest

In the jungle, monkeys swing,
Poking fun at everything.
A parrot squawks a silly joke,
While a sloth just takes a poke.

Vines are tangled, like my hair,
Bees buzzing without a care.
A toucan with a goofy grin,
Sipping nectar, trying to win.

Frogs in hats, each one a star,
Dance around, they're quite bizarre.
Lizards laugh and join the play,
Cheering on a sloth's ballet.

Nature's mischief fills the air,
Every critter seems to dare.
In this place, the laughter flows,
Where wildness blooms and joy just grows.

Footprints in the Soft Sand

Steps mark the beach, a silly trail,
A crab is plotting, setting sail.
With tiny legs, it scuttles by,
Making plans, oh me, oh my!

A seagull swoops with quite a flair,
Stealing snacks that folks lay bare.
We chase it down, but it just laughs,
Running fast on tiny calfs.

Kids are digging, castles tall,
While waves rise up and start to fall.
Sandy faces all around,
In this fun where joy is found.

As the sun dips, skies turn pink,
We share a giggle, a wink, a clink.
Footprints washed by the sea's embrace,
Leave behind this happy space.

When the Stars Dance Above the Sea

Stars twinkle, doing a jig,
The moon joins in, all nice and big.
While crabs throw a late-night bash,
With tiny hats, they boogie, flash!

Waves whisper secrets to the shore,
As dolphins laugh and swim some more.
Each splash is like a silly cheer,
Echoes of joy we hold so dear.

Shells roll in on a playful spree,
Requesting all to join their glee.
Sandcastles bow to the mighty night,
While the crickets chirp their delight.

Beneath the stars, the fun won't cease,
Every moment wraps in peace.
With laughter soaring, spirits high,
We dance like stars across the sky.

The Melody of Rippling Waves

Waves whisper tunes along the shore,
Telling tales of adventures galore.
A fish with shades sings out of tune,
While seaweed dances to the tune.

Each roll of the sea, a funny beat,
Crabs express it with tiny feet.
Seashells chime, a quirky band,
Swaying gently, hand in hand.

Seagulls squawk, adding to the song,
While turtles nod, agreeing all along.
A playful dolphin leaps with flair,
Belly flops, splashes everywhere!

As the sun sets, the music fades,
Yet laughter from this world cascades.
In this symphony, joy is sane,
Echoing softly, like gentle rain.

Cherished Moments in Coastal Bliss

Sandy toes and sunburned nose,
Pineapple drinks, the perfect pose.
Seagulls squawk, they steal our fries,
We laugh as they fly, oh what a surprise!

Chasing crabs, a silly sight,
Falling over, oh what a fright.
Beach balls bouncing, kids all scream,
Life's a beach, or so it seems!

Sunset hues, a vibrant dance,
We trip on waves, oh what a chance!
A volleyball flies, we duck and weave,
In this paradise, we truly believe!

Laughter echoes, a joyful sound,
Making memories, all around.
With each splash and silly grin,
We're sun-kissed, happy, let the fun begin!

Life's Mosaic in Tropical Colors

Painted skies of bright cascade,
See the toucans, they invade!
Sipping punch, we toast with glee,
Who knew fruit could be so free?

Swaying palms with cheeky grin,
They tease the breeze, let the fun begin!
Dancing lizards, moving fast,
Wonder what they had for breakfast?

Seashell hunts, our treasure quest,
Each one's unique, it's simply the best.
Flip-flops flying as we sprint,
"Is that your shoe?" Oh, what a hint!

Boys with surfboards, quite the sight,
Wipeouts happen, oh what a fright!
With laughter echoing all around,
In this vibrant place, joy is found!

Floating Lanterns in the Moonlight

Underneath the moon's best glow,
Lanterns float where soft winds blow.
Frogs croak tunes, a country fair,
While mockingbirds serenade the air.

Dancing shadows on the sand,
We twirl and leap, oh isn't it grand?
Our feast of snacks is quite a sight,
Those chips won't last, they're in for a fight!

Catch a lantern, say your wish,
Though yours might be a tasty dish!
Giggles echo, splashes fly,
Who knew the sea could make us high?

As the night comes to a close,
We'll never forget the goofy pose.
Under stars, we'll drift and sway,
Memories made, come what may!

Canopy of Dreams Above the Sea

High above, the branches sway,
Chasing squirrels who laugh and play.
Tropical fruits both ripe and sweet,
We munch and giggle, a tasty treat.

Beneath the boughs, we find our space,
Playing hide and seek, oh, what a race!
With each discovery, fits of laughter,
In this wild hideaway, joy is what we're after!

Parrots squawk, they mimic our calls,
They tease and taunt, such feathered brawls.
Swinging low, we feel so free,
Under this leafy canopy.

As sunset paints the skies with cheer,
We share our dreams, oh so near.
With hearts so light, we dive and dive,
In this big world, we truly thrive!

Sun-Kissed Reflections

Oh, the sun's a jolly prankster,
It dances on my nose like cheese.
With every splash, our laughter grows,
I swear, it's tickling the breeze.

The coconut tree winks at me,
As I trip on a flip-flop prank.
Sandy toes and salty smiles,
In this beachty, quirky prank.

We play tag with the seagulls bold,
While crabs declare a race on land.
Each wave's a joke, each splash a laugh,
In this paradise, we're so unplanned.

But when the tide rolls out to sleep,
And shells gather secrets to share,
We'll launch our giggles to the stars,
And float our dreams upon the air.

Vibrant Echoes of Paradise

In this place where colors burst,
The flowers throw a wild party.
They hum and twirl like tipsy bees,
Is it pollen? No, just hearty!

A toucan's squawk is jokes galore,
With every crop of fruit, we cheer.
The monkeys swing and drop their toys,
I think they're drinking from our beer.

The sunset's painted with silly hues,
Each shade a grin from sky to sea.
We gather for a beachside feast,
Where laughter's served like coconut tea.

And when the night drapes its velvet cape,
The stars begin their stand-up show.
So grab your drink and join the fun,
In this vibrant echo of glow.

Whispering Palms at Dusk

The palms are giggling under stars,
As crickets play their late-night tune.
A lizard scales the garden wall,
With swagger that could make a raccoon swoon.

The ocean's laugh rolls to the shore,
Where we watch fish fashioning socks.
They dance along the water's edge,
In shoes made of colorful rocks.

But wait! The sunset's lost its hat,
A flamingo stirs it with a peck.
We chuckle as the night slips in,
And chill with drinks to catch a wreck.

So here we sit, where laughter flows,
Among the whispering, lively leaves.
In this vibrant, chuckling paradise,
We find the joy that never leaves.

Twilight in the Coral Gardens

In twilight where the fish wear hats,
Coral reefs share their tales of glee.
They giggle under the moonlit waves,
While turtles rock out at the marquee.

With snorkels as our jester's caps,
We dive into the coral's smile.
Every splash sings a silly song,
And we chuckle in our watery style.

We dance with dolphins, twirl with eels,
Each bubble pops like giggles bright.
A sea star waves its quirky arms,
As crabs get loose and join the night.

So let the moonlight sparkle so,
With every wave, a joke's been penned.
In coral gardens, fun's the plan,
Where laughter's tide will never end.

Tides of Tranquility and Wonder

Beneath the palm, a crab takes a stroll,
It dances sideways, aiming for a roll.
A seagull chuckles, quite full of glee,
Stealing a fry, the ocean's his spree.

Waves lap like puppies, playful and bright,
While fishermen nap, dreaming of a bite.
The sun winks down, like it's got a treat,
Shells whisper secrets of sandy retreat.

Sandcastles crumbling, they wave goodbye,
To a mighty wave that makes little kids cry.
But laughter echoes, a fun-loving sound,
As everyone searches for joy all around.

When night descends, in a starry dance,
The tiki torches sway, inviting a chance.
To join the fiesta, it's all quite absurd,
With coconut drinks and antics unheard.

Down by the Water's Edge

By the shore, a dog takes a dive,
Chasing a wave, oh look, he's alive!
Kids giggle loud, constructing their fate,
A bucket and spade, their castle awaits.

Flip-flops forgotten, as feet run free,
Chasing the tide, how tasty is sea!
A clam waves, as if in a jest,
While seaweed tickles the little ones' quest.

Beach balls bounce, a riotous cheer,
As Uncle Bob trips, spilling his beer.
The ice cream melts, dripping with glee,
Right on the nose of his old blimp of a knees.

As sunset paints colors mixed in a jar,
Friends gather round, strumming guitars.
With laughter and song, the day's nearly done,
In a world where the sea and humor are one.

The Pulse of the Tropical Night

A breeze carries giggles, alive in the air,
As fireflies twinkle, showing they care.
The moon smiles down, a grand old fellow,
While crickets compose, a chorus so mellow.

Coconut drinks served with little umbrellas,
The parrot gets tipsy, reciting his tellas.
Sand underfoot feels like a warm hug,
As friends share stories, all snug like a bug.

Dancing shadows playing tag with the light,
While someone steps on a flip-flop too tight.
With laughter erupting, joy flies around,
Underneath palm trees, where silliness is found.

The night rolls on, with stars burning bright,
A playful reminder of fun's pure delight.
As laughter fades out, like the last glowing spark,
The heart of the island, alive in the dark.

Secrets of Sun and Shade

In the cool of the shade, a lizard just grins,
While sunbathers sweat, as the heat slowly wins.
Picnics are tasty, with ants on the hunt,
They carry away crumbs, the tiny gaunt stunt.

Chairs tilted back, where folks fall asleep,
With dreams of coconuts and treasures to keep.
While the breeze sneaks in, tickling noses,
The gardener laughs, he knows how it dozes.

They splash and they play, thrown in the air,
As the sun turns up, with no hint of a care.
Hats flying high, like flags in a breeze,
As everyone laughs, feeling quite at ease.

An octopus watches, curious and sly,
While beachgoers joke, and the day passes by.
As day turns to night, and the fun's almost done,
In this world of warmth, we all just have fun.

Jewel-Toned Waters and Leaves

Oh, the water is a bright blue,
With leaves that giggle in the breeze.
A fish in shades of pink goes woohoo,
While turtles dance among the trees.

The lizards wear their finest hues,
They prance and pose on waterfalls.
The drinks come served with fancy straws,
And seagulls might just steal your calls.

The crab's a waiter at the beach,
He winks and offers shells with style.
The sand is ticklish at your feet,
Where every grain can make you smile.

In this paradise of colorful shows,
Even the coconuts laugh and quake.
So grab a float and off you go,
To join the fun, for fun's own sake!

Radiance of Island Heritage

A dance of colors in the sun,
Where legends twirl like palm trees sway.
Old stories spread like laughter spun,
In every wave they sing and play.

The parrots gossip 'neath the shade,
While flowers burst in hues so bright.
Grandma's recipes are lovingly made,
And every bite just feels so right.

The drums are thumping, feet are light,
As mongoose race for coconut treats.
The laughter echoed through the night,
While everyone indulges in sweets.

Here, heritage is a sunny song,
With every twist there's a little cheer.
So come along and sing along,
You'll find good vibes and no fear!

Shimmering Paths Through Lush Wilderness

The jungle paths are winding dreams,
Where monkeys swing and parakeets squawk.
A garden blooms with funny themes,
As nature plays a funny walk.

The sloths take naps on branches high,
While frogs proclaim a concert grand.
The vines all twist like ropes in tie,
Creating a jungle band so planned.

While waterfalls go splashing loud,
The scenery gives everyone glee.
Even the clouds hang a bit proud,
As if they want to join the spree.

So wander through this vibrant scene,
With laughter echoing like a tune.
Each step a joy, a sight unseen,
In this wild and wacky afternoon!

Flickering Fireflies in Twilight Nooks

As the sun dips low, the stars awake,
Fireflies twinkle like they're in a game.
Dancing around with each little shake,
It's a chase of lights, not one the same.

The crickets cheer with their sweet song,
While shadows play hide and seek pranks.
It's in this magic, time feels wrong,
With giggles echoing, heartfelt thanks.

The children chase the glow with glee,
Their laughter dances through the night.
In every nook a mystery,
With fireflies leading joys in flight.

So flutter along the glowing trails,
As the night whispers tales untold.
In these bright moments, love prevails,
Where every glimmer shines so bold.

Ocean's Breath in a Sultry Night

The waves sing a silly tune,
Beneath the bright and blushing moon.
A crab dances with such flair,
While fish gossip without a care.

Jellyfish waltz with graceful ease,
While parrots squawk in the palm trees.
A coconut rolls down the shore,
As locals laugh and ask for more.

Sandcastles rise, then swiftly fall,
Seagulls join in with a squawky call.
On this beach, all worries flee,
What a sight! Oh, can't you see?

In the night, the stars align,
Cocktails spill, their colors shine.
The ocean breathes, a funny sight,
As laughter carries through the night.

Echoes of Laughter Amidst the Foliage

In the jungle, vines twist and shout,
Monkeys swing and jump about.
A toucan's beak is quite a sight,
While snakes giggle in delight.

Leaves rustle with a cheeky breeze,
As lizards play hide and seek with ease.
A sloth grins from a cameo,
While frogs sing tunes, their voices low.

Beneath the palms, the fun unfolds,
Each story shared, a joy retold.
The sun peeks through, all golden bright,
And every moment feels just right.

Echoes of laughter fill the air,
In this haven, life has flair.
With every giggle, joy ignites,
In lush green lands, hearts take flight.

Unveiling the Spirit of the Tropics

In colorful shirts and crazy hats,
We dance with rhythm, just like cats.
A parrot squawks, "What's the plan?"
To beachside bars, we scamper, man!

Pineapples grin while coconuts cheer,
As locals toast with a joyous beer.
The rhythm of life beats strong and bright,
With every step, we feel the light.

A limbo stick waits, so let's try,
Falling over while dodging a pie.
Laughter echoes through the sand,
Life's a party, so dance hand in hand.

In every smile and silly jest,
The spirit shines, it's truly blessed.
Let's not unveil what's tucked away—
Just laugh and play, come what may!

Kisses of Warm Ocean Air

Warm breezes tease the frizzy hair,
While flip-flops flop without a care.
A seagull snatches fries from a plate,
As blunders ensue—what a fate!

The sun-kissed sand tickles the feet,
Under skies where bright colors meet.
With a splash, someone jumps too high,
And we all laugh till we cry.

Margaritas swirl, their flavors bold,
Each sip promises a story told.
We twirl and dance, letting worries go,
Embracing the magic of the flow.

With a wink, the ocean sighs,
As laughter echoes through the skies.
Here's to moments, sweet and rare,
Blessed by kisses of warm ocean air.

Luminous Waves of Paradise

The waves dance bright and bold,
Splashing colors, pure gold.
Seagulls squawk as they dive in,
Trying hard to catch a fin.

Beach balls bounce, they fly away,
Chasing sunlight, come what may.
Sandy feet leave a trail of laughs,
Caught in games and silly gaffes.

A crab snaps quick at my toe,
I jump and giggle: "Oh no, oh no!"
Sunsets toast with drinks in hand,
Sipping coconut in soft, warm sand.

Joy abounds in every wave,
From surfboard spills to sandcastles brave.
Laughter bubbles underneath,
In this golden land beneath.

Glistening Canopy Dreams

Beneath the leaves, we twirl and sway,
Monkeys watch us dance and play.
A toucan laughs, what a funny sight,
As he squawks his birdy delight.

The trees wear hats made of mist,
While I try to climb, I twist and twist.
Vines are swinging, I trip and tumble,
Snickers and giggles, oh how I fumble!

Lizards lounge, they have no care,
While I'm dodging the bugs in the air.
Jumping with joy at the sight of a breeze,
Pineapple smoothies are sure to please!

In this leafy, lively spree,
Every moment's a comedy!
Nature's stage has me in stitches,
Flora's antics are just pure riches.

Radiant Flora at Dusk

Petals bursting, colors bright,
Dancing softly, oh what a sight!
Bees zoom by with a bumble cheer,
Trying ever so hard to steer.

The sun dips low, it's time to play,
Flowers open, come join the fray!
I trip on roots and land with a thud,
Echoes of laughter, or is that a dud?

A butterfly lands on my nose,
I sneeze and it frantically goes!
"Please stay put!" I plead with a grin,
While the fireflies chuckle, then join in.

In the garden of silly sights,
Every petal hosts joyful nights.
Nature giggles in vibrant bloom,
As I dance with flowers, weaving my loom.

Tropical Reflections

Mirrors of water, bright and full,
Splashing about, they play the fool.
Fish giggle in their wet parade,
With fins that flip like a masquerade.

My hat flies off, caught in the breeze,
Running after it, with such wild glee!
A parrot squawks, "You've lost your style!"
I bow to it, wearing a smile.

Breezes tease with a gentle brush,
Turtles chuckle, causing a hush.
I join their lane, moving so slow,
Giggling and wobbling, off we go!

Reflections dance as laughter rings,
Nature's chorus with bright little sings.
In this paradise, all things collide,
With joy in the heart, let's take a ride!

Evanescent Moments by the Shore

Waves wiggle and dance with glee,
A crab steals my sandwich, oh me!
Seagulls squawk a comical song,
I chase them down the beach, oh so wrong.

Flip-flops fly in a sudden gust,
The sunscreen bottle, a little bust,
I slip and slide, just like a pro,
Turned beach ballet into a show!

A child builds castles, then they fall,
My ice cream drips—oh, such a brawl!
Laughter echoes, the sun sets low,
These fleeting moments, a delightful flow.

With salty hair and joy in tow,
I ponder life, on this vibrant glow.
Each tickling wave brings a new grin,
A treasure of laughter, where to begin?

Luminous Tides and Tropical Vibes

At dawn, a parrot steals my hat,
It seems to think it's cool as a cat!
The beach ball bounces, oh what a sight,
I chase it down, with all my might.

Shells and starfish play hide and seek,
A fish swims by, judging my physique,
I wave to dolphins, they laugh and jump,
While I trip over my own big clump.

Bikinis and board shorts, a colorful blend,
Sandy toes giggle, the fun never bends,
Ice-cold coconuts bring sweet relief,
While my friend's sunburn turns into a chief!

As shadows stretch and evening glows,
I dance barefoot, flaunting my toes.
These playful moments, how they delight,
Under tropical skies, everything feels right.

A Symphony of Sunlight and Shadow

An orchestra of crickets begins to play,
While I stumble over my towel, oh hey!
The palm trees whisper a funny tale,
As an iguana sneaks in without fail.

Sunbeams prance with a zesty cheer,
While I sip my drink, not a drop to spare,
A flip-flop flings into the air,
Greeted by laughter from those who care.

My beach chair wobbles, a mischievous toss,
I wave like a fish, my balance a loss,
The ocean giggles, a bubbly tease,
As I dive for my shades, lost in the breeze.

At twilight, the crabs host a grand show,
While I sip my punch, in fluorescent glow.
These moments of laughter, rarely confined,
In this vibrant world, oh how we unwind!

Hidden Wonders Under the Canopy

The jungle whispers, what will I find?
A monkey laughs, not far behind!
Bananas dangle from the trees,
As I stumble through, trying to appease.

Frogs croak tunes, so offbeat and sweet,
While I trip on roots, stumbling on my feet.
A parrot shouts, 'You're about to slip!'
I grin and chuckle, my jokes often trip.

Bright flowers giggle, swaying in cheer,
While bugs throw a rave, never fear!
I dance with shadows, a confusing game,
But nature applauds, it loves my fame.

As dusk wraps this tale in a cloak,
I laugh at the rain, a wet little joke.
These hidden wonders, both wild and bold,
Make great tales, endlessly told!

Dazzling Shallows of the Sea

In the shallows, fish do dance,
With silly fins, they take a chance.
Crabs wear hats, slightly askew,
Underwater parties, all for you.

Seashells gossip, oh what a sight,
Telling tales of their salty plight.
An octopus plays piano tunes,
While jellyfish float, swaying with spoons.

Starfish break into a quick jig,
As the seahorse leads, looking big.
The dolphins giggle, racing near,
All in fun, with nothing to fear.

A clam with dreams of being a star,
Tries to sing, but gets quite bizarre.
While shrimp hold concerts in the sand,
Their tiny voices, a rock band!

Illuminated Trails of the Night

Bats wear capes, zooming around,
While owls hoot, making quite the sound.
Fireflies flash like tiny stars,
Lighting up the night like bizarre cars.

A raccoon sneaks, searching for snacks,
His little paws, oh what a max!
In the moonlight, shadows prance,
Everyone's invited to this dance.

The frogs croak jokes on lily pads,
While toads play cards, driving the lads.
As laughter echoes through the trees,
The night's alive with playful breeze.

When the sun peeks, all creatures hide,
As bedtime stories come with pride.
But in dreams, they dance and play,
Ready for another funny day!

Serene Glare of Coastal Bliss

A coconut rolls down the beach,
Chasing waves, oh what a reach!
Seagulls squawk, sharing a treat,
Finding treasures, it can't be beat.

Sandcastles rise, a noble quest,
Built by kids who never rest.
A crab becomes a king for fun,
Wearing shells, he shouts, "I've won!"

Surfers tumble, have no fear,
The waves don't mind, they simply cheer.
Beach balls bounce, what a great sight,
With laughter mixed in the sunlight.

Beach umbrellas tilt in the breeze,
While sunscreen's slapped across all knees.
The day fades, laughter rings,
Tomorrow brings more silly things!

Chasing Sunbeams in the Jungle

Monkeys swing with goofy grins,
Chasing sunbeams, oh where it spins!
Parrots squawk, a comic show,
In the jungle, there's a vibrant glow.

Tigers sneak with playful paws,
Pouncing on bugs, then taking a pause.
Lemurs play, leaping high,
Making funny faces, oh my, oh my!

The cake of mud is a favorite treat,
Frogs jump in, it can't be beat.
Snakes do the twist, wiggling free,
Dancing wildly, just wait and see!

Vines swing low, bananas drop,
With every tumble, they can't stop.
In this jungle, there's fun galore,
Each day brings laughter, who could ask for more?

An Oasis of Warmth and Delight

In the sun's embrace, we jest,
Cocktails sloshing like a fest.
Coconuts grin upon the shore,
Crabs tap dance, who could ask for more?

Flip-flops squeak, the humor flows,
As seagulls squawk in silly throes.
Palm trees wave, they know the score,
Whispers of laughter, legends galore.

With beach balls bouncing in the air,
Sunburnt noses, a comical flair.
We chase the waves, it's all a game,
In this paradise, we're all the same.

Sandcastles crumbled, sprinkle of glee,
Living life's absurdity is key.
Under the sun, we're light as a kite,
In this cheerful land, everything's bright.

Glimpses of the Island's Soul

Under starry skies, we gather round,
Stories and giggles are easily found.
A mongoose slips, it tumbles and rolls,
While we're busy searching for lost shoals.

Lizards strut in their flashy attire,
Like tiny models, they never tire.
Bananas laughing as they sway,
Even the fruit wants to join in the play.

The breeze is naughty, it tickles and chokes,
As palm leaves dance, like cheeky folks.
We sip on drinks that are too sweet to take,
But who cares? It's all about the shake!

In this realm where humor resides,
Joy runs free like ocean tides.
With giggles echoing beneath the moon,
We find our heart's island, a whimsical tune.

The Call of the Exotic and Unknown

Foreign smells swirl, a curious tease,
Tropical fruits, oh what a wheeze!
A parrot squawks in a pirate's jest,
"Who needs a map? I know best!"

Dancing shadows in the fading light,
Chasing tales and lost delight.
A coconut falls — thud on my head,
I laugh so hard, I forget what I said.

Mysterious noises from the palm trees,
Jungle spirits playing tricks with ease.
Colorful fish in a flip-flop race,
Who knew aquatic games could be such a chase?

With every splash, a chuckle erupts,
As laughter bubbles, we all erupt.
In this realm of exotic flair,
We find ourselves without a care.

Tapestry of Lush Green Dreams

Ferny whispers weave through the trees,
Silly monkeys swinging like they're on keys.
The jungle bursts with giggles and glee,
While sloths take their time, they make it a spree.

With paintbrush sunsets splashed in the sky,
We joke 'bout the clouds as they drift by.
Avocado faces give us a grin,
As we plop on the grass, absurd as sin.

Parrots crack jokes, "What's your best line?"
"Come join the adventure, a sip of the brine!"
The breeze carries laughter from all corners,
In this lively patch, we're true performers.

In a patchwork quilt of joyous mirth,
We find our place, our happy berth.
With every giggle, the world seems bright,
In this verdant haven, all feels right.

Glowing Horizons

The sun wears shades, quite sly,
While seagulls dance, oh my, oh my!
A crab in flip-flops, such a sight,
He scuttles by in pure delight.

A rooster struts with quite the flair,
In colorful gear, he rules the square.
The beachfront's alive with laughter loud,
It's party time! Join the crowd.

Iridescent Sunlit Shores

The sandcastles lean, too high to stand,
While kids throw buckets, grains of sand.
A fish in sunglasses swims with grace,
Saying, 'Sun's out! Let's pick up the pace!'

The beach ball bounces—what a game!
Someone shouts, 'That was my claim to fame!'
Yet jellyfish lounge in their own way,
Wishing they too could join the fray.

Echoes of Celestial Breezes

Palm trees sway in a dance so bold,
While a toucan tells tales, all retold.
The breeze whispers secrets, just to tease,
As sun hats fly off like leaves in the breeze.

An iguana in a sunhat takes a stroll,
Avoiding flip-flops, that's his goal.
A coconut rolls, it's not polite,
As laughter erupts, what a funny sight!

Vibrant Tides and Whispering Palms

The waves clap back in playful strife,
While surfers compete for a splashy life.
With laughter and jokes, the tide rolls in,
As starfish cheer, 'Let the fun begin!'

A parrot crows, 'You've got this!' loud,
While tourists try not to look too proud.
Then plop! A splash from the boat nearby,
As someone yells, 'My drink says goodbye!'

In the Embrace of Verdant Giants

Under trees so tall and wide,
Monkeys swing, a playful ride.
Parrots squawk with colors bright,
Dancing leaves in morning light.

Lizards lounging, chests puffed out,
Claiming sun spots, what a clout!
Frogs join in with ribbits loud,
While ants march in a proud crowd.

Bouncing from a branch so free,
A toucan drops, health bars for me!
Sipping fruit drinks, feeling fine,
I dream of a life divine.

But slipping on a juicy peel,
Oh dear! I lose my balanced feel!
The jungle giggles at my fall,
In this green world, we all have a ball.

Waves Washing Away Whispered Sorrows

Seagulls laugh and take a dive,
While beach balls bounce, it's a busy hive.
Sandcastles built with such delight,
Towers collapse in a wave's might.

Flip-flops flying as kids run near,
Splashing water, raucous cheer!
Sunburned noses, red as a glow,
Flip and flop like fish in tow.

A crab scuttles, slides with flair,
Challenging toes unaware.
I trip on my towel with a shout,
Ow! How did I end up faced out?

The ocean laughs, it's quite a scene,
A madcap dance in shades of green.
Even the waves seem to giggle,
As I do my best to wriggle.

A Garden of Sweet Indulgence

Beneath a tree that drips with glee,
Mangoes call, 'Come, eat with me!'
Papaya slices sweet and bright,
Fruit flies buzz, oh what a sight!

Banana peels peel back with zest,
But slip on them? It's no jest!
Berries tumble in a race,
Splat! Melon seeds all over the place!

Coconut drummers keep the beat,
While pineapples drop a fruity treat.
Sipping juice like royalty,
Sticky fingers full of glee.

But the wasps join in, what a shock!
Turning sweet treats into a bock!
In this garden wild, fun's the theme,
Just watch your snack, it seems, they scheme!

Prismatic Reflections in Tropical Waters

Beneath the sun, fish dance in glee,
Their scales like disco balls, you see!
A turtle floats, quite proud, you'll find,
Wearing a shell that's stylishly designed.

Crabs scuttle sideways, they strut with flair,
"Look at me!" they boast without a care.
In underwater threads, they throw a bash,
While seaweed sways in a funky flash.

The coral reef sports its brightest dress,
A rainbow of colors, we must confess!
Octopuses juggle, what a sight to behold,
They're the clowns of the sea, bold and old.

With each wave crashing, laughter erupts,
Nature's own party as joy interrupts.
In this vibrant realm where silliness reigns,
The ocean sings sweetly, its heart never wanes.

Kaleidoscope of Flora and Waves.

Bamboo hats bob, see them go!
In the breeze, they dance, a funny show.
Flowers wearing hats, who would have guessed?
Blooming with laughter, they feel quite blessed.

Coconuts giggle, round like a ball,
They roll down hills, have a tropical brawl.
Bright parrots gossip, chatters and caws,
Sharing stories of squirrelly paws.

Palms sway like they're at a grand soirée,
While the mangoes drop, like fruit confetti play!
In gardens where laughter is always awake,
The sunflowers wink, for fun's own sake.

Underneath the leaves, a lizard prances,
In plaid pajamas, he takes his chances.
Nature's circus, alive in delight,
Where silly surprises await every night.

Beneath the Lush Canopy

The jungle's alive, with giggles and sighs,
Monkeys trade jokes, filling up the skies.
Parrots wear glasses, look oh-so-fly,
Reading the leaves, they give it a try.

Frogs sing ballads, their voices quite grand,
While beetles perform, the best rock band.
A chameleon joins, but look and behold,
He changes colors that are too bold!

Snakes on a vine, doing a twist,
Making a racket, you can't help but miss!
In this green theatre, the fun never stops,
Every leaf giggles, every branch hops.

As shadows dance under the vibrant light,
The forest's a party, an endless night.
With every rustle, there's humor to find,
In nature's embrace, we all are entwined.

Waves of Sapphire Dreams

Surfboards parade, all lined up in style,
Riders do tricks, with laughter and smiles.
Wave after wave, they tumble and roll,
Splashing freedom, that's how they stroll.

Sandcastles built, adorned with flair,
A prince and a princess, they just don't care.
Seagulls squawk jokes, they're quite the jest,
While crabs throw a party, they're nature's best.

Mermaids lounge on the shores, looking chic,
Swapping fish tales and laughing unique.
Dolphins leap high, their tricks bring delight,
Playing tag with the stars in the soft moonlight.

As sunsets paint skies, they giggle and sigh,
The ocean whispers secrets, oh my oh my!
In waves of laughter, they all find their groove,
A joyful escape, where spirits improve.

Palette of Paradise: Nature's Canvas

In colors bright, the birds all sing,
Green leaves dance, while coconuts swing.
A parrot's joke, it's quite a sight,
He says, "Why did the palm tree take flight?"

With paint so bold, the flowers grin,
They paint the world with cheeky spin.
A tulip whispers, 'Look at me!
I've got more flair than any bee!'

Waves crash gently, with splashes near,
The clumsy fish, they cause a cheer.
They trip and tumble, what a show,
All hail the clownfish, the bobbing pro!

So grab your brush, let's make a splash,
In this wild world, there's no need to dash.
With laughter bright, we paint the sky,
The canvas of joy, oh me, oh my!

Breezes Carrying Tropical Sweetness

The wind brings laughter, oh what a tease,
It tickles noses, sways the trees.
"Why did the breeze forget its hat?"
Because it thought it looked like a bat!

Coconuts giggle, bouncing down,
As if they're kings, wearing a crown.
They plop and roll, a game of chance,
"Watch out! It's the fruit's dance dance dance!"

Pirates chase whispers of sweet coconuts,
Stumbling and mumbling, oh look at those nuts!
They swing from vines, a comical sight,
"Yo ho ho, where's my sword?" in plight!

A breeze bursts forth, with jokes in tow,
It sails on by, putting on a show.
As laughter flows and giggles soar,
The balmy air begs for just one more!

Reflections on Calm Water

The water winks, a mirror so sly,
It shows a fish with a very big eye.
"Why did you stare?" the fish exclaimed,
"I'm just checking if my scales are famed!"

Ripples giggle as they break the glass,
A frog jumps in with a floppy sass.
"Hey buddy, why the long leap?
Because the last one made me lose sleep!"

Beneath the surface, the turtles glide,
They whisper jokes as they take a ride.
"Why was the sea snail late for class?
I'm too slow, oh what a mess!"

In reflections wild, laughter is found,
In waters deep, with joy all around.
As fish flip-flop and frolic with glee,
The calm water's life is the best comedy!

Explorations of Island Dreams

We set out on a quest, full of glee,
With ice cream cones, and sand as our spree.
The map said treasure; what did it mean?
Turned out it was a bowl of whipped cream!

Palm trees sway, they join our fun,
"Who brought the sunscreen? This isn't a run!"
With sunburned noses and sandy toes,
We laugh at life, that's how it goes!

A crab in a hat, oh what a find,
He clicks his claws, oh so refined.
"Why do crabs never share their food?
Because they're shellfish, dude, how rude!"

As laughter fills the balmy air,
We make memories without a care.
Exploring dreams of laughter and sun,
In our island world, oh what a run!

Luster of the Exotic Canopy

In the jungle, a parrot squawks,
Racing by on its wobbly talks.
A toucan trips on a leafy vine,
Sipping nectar, thinking it's fine.

Monkeys leap, a clumsy display,
Dropping fruit in a breezy way.
Lizards laugh at the giant frog,
While he croaks like a groggy dog.

Dappled Light on Sandy Paths

Footprints dance in the golden sand,
One's a crab, the other's a hand.
Flip-flops flying in the summer breeze,
As tourists giggle, losing their keys.

A sunburnt tourist takes a dive,
Only to land with a graceful jive.
Seagulls snicker at each slip,
While the waves weave a silly trip.

Secrets Beneath the Emerald Waves

A fish in shades of fluorescent hue,
Keeps asking, 'What's a hook to do?'
While mermaids giggle at their tail,
Even dolphins can't help but flail.

Coral reefs share tales of the sea,
Of clams that sing in glee,
And crabs that dance with delight,
Each moonlit romp is a comical sight.

Glittering Dusk Over Coral Reefs

As the sun bids the day goodbye,
Starfish throw a party, oh my!
With disco balls made of sea foam,
While turtles rave, feeling at home.

A clownfish tells a knock-knock joke,
Causing even the dolphins to choke.
Bubbles rise in a giggling spree,
Under the waves, all blithe and free.

Hearts Entwined in Golden Light

Under the sun, we dance so bright,
Boys in grass skirts, quite the sight!
Swaying to rhythms, a giggly delight,
Even the coconuts are feeling the bite.

Laughter erupts from a splashing wave,
As we try to surf, oh, who needs a cave?
The sand sticks tight, but we're feeling brave,
In this golden glow, we misbehave.

With snacks on our minds, we hunt for eats,
Bananas and mangoes, oh, what sweet treats!
We juggle the fruits, slip on our feet,
Tropical bliss can't be beat.

As the sun dips low, our giggles combine,
With friends at our side, we're feeling divine.
In the glow of the dusk, we sip on our wine,
Hearts entwined sweetly, like a perfect line.

Fleeting Moments in the Tropical Realm

Palm trees are waving, a comical show,
One falls for our hat, oh no! Oh no!
We chase our belongings, moving too slow,
In this banana land, we steal the flow.

A toucan flies by, what a funny parade,
It's flirting with lizards, quite a charade.
Sunburnt and giggling, our worries all fade,
With a splash from the waves, our worries delayed.

Catch the sunset, quick! It's a running race,
Tripping on sandals, oh, what a disgrace!
With smiles so wide, we roll in the space,
Fleeting moments, we're lost in the chase.

As nightfall descends, we feast on a treat,
Grilled bugs on skewers, now that's something sweet!
With laughter and joy, our travel elite,
Moments like these? We're feeling complete.

Celestial Dance on Vibrant Horizons

Bright stars are our partners, take a twirl!
Belly flops abound; oh, give it a whirl!
In this cosmic bash, watch the colors unfurl,
Our feet full of sand, we spin and we hurl.

Even the crabs join the night's funky beat,
They sidestep in rhythms, all in good heat.
With coconuts flying, it's quite the retreat,
Laughter and moonlight, oh, what a feat!

Sneaking some snacks while avoiding the waves,
The seaweed brigade, so sneaky, it braves.
Each bite a chuckle, like fools on the staves,
In this dance of the night, wild spirit it saves.

As the sun peeks up, we beg it to stay,
Bearing our secrets, the night will not sway.
With dreams tied in laughter, come what may,
A celestial dance, always on display.

Treasures Hidden Among the Leaves

In a jungle of quirks, treasures abound,
A pineapple crown, who'd wear it around?
Fungi in costumes, fun sights to be found,
Leaves whisper secrets, in laughter they're bound.

Shrimp in a party, they're shaking their tails,
Our giggles explode as the laughter prevails.
With each tiny critter, mischief entails,
Chasing butterflies, we follow their trails.

A hammock of dreams sways lightly above,
Tangled in laughter, we feel the love.
Jokes on the breeze, like a push from a glove,
Searching for treasures, the kind you dream of.

With snacks stashed away, and dancing that frees,
We treasure these moments, no need for keys,
Among ripe coconuts, and buzzing bees,
Adventures await, in the rustling leaves.

www.ingramcontent.com/pod-product-compliance
Lightning Source LLC
Chambersburg PA
CBHW072120070526
44585CB00016B/1513